The Little Book of
BOLLOX
DETOX

GW00514801

The Little Book of

BOLLOX DETOX

'NO PAIN = NO PAIN'

MIKE ANDERIESZ
JASMINE BIRTLES

B☘XTREE

First published 2002 by Boxtree
an imprint of Pan Macmillan Ltd
Pan Macmillan, 20 New Wharf Road, London N1 9RR
Basingstoke and Oxford
Associated companies throughout the world
www.panmacmillan.com

ISBN 0 7522 6153 3

1 3 5 7 9 8 6 4 2

A CIP catalogue record for this book is available from
the British Library.

Design by Dan Newman/Perfect Bound Ltd
Printed by Bath Press Ltd, Bath

The authors of this book have turned their lives around in the past three months. How? That's the secret they want to share with YOU!

To those who say, 'Detoxing your body is the key to reinvigorating your soul', we say Bollox. This book will prove that you can lead a better life, enjoy Tantric-style sex and defy the aging process while smoking twenty fags a day and eating enough fried food to scare Colonel Sanders. We can demonstrate how any fitness fad can be faked and any beauty product knocked up for under a fiver. In fact, if you are not totally satisfied with the results, we challenge you to write a better self-help book, get it published and send us 10 per cent of the royalties – that's how confident we are.

And remember, it's not what goes into your body that counts, it's how inexpensively you can flush it out! Do it the *Bollox Detox* way – after all, you did buy the book, so you might as well, eh?

Glossary

Confused by all the terms? Here are a few crap-free definitions for a healthier lifestyle.

Toxins – what's left over from that evening where you had such a good time you woke up on a plane to Marrakech.

Low-fat – what manufacturers put on food that has so many additives in it there's no room for fat or any actual nutrition.

Low-calorie – what manufacturers put on food that has had all the substance, taste and texture artificially removed.

Supplement – the pill you can take so that you can continue drinking and smoking and still think you're healthy.

Acceptable weight – at least two stone less than whatever you are now.

Unhealthy – what thin people call you if you're fat and what fat people call you if you're thin.

Snacking – food eaten in between meals that somehow doesn't include calories.

Cellulite – proof that when you've hit the bottom it *can* get worse.

Nutritious – green.

Healthy eating – green.

Green – green.

Fibre-rich – something that looks and tastes a bit like Bruce Forsyth's hairpiece.

Diuretic – God's antidote to junk food: fast in, fast out.

E₃ Oils – so boring they make cod-liver oil look like an aphrodisiac.

Cholesterol – invented by the CIA to give fat people something to blame instead of their own lack of willpower.

Organic – unwashed.

Vegetarian – a skinny person who does not eat meat.

Vegan – a very skinny person who hardly eats anything.

Cannibal – a well-fed person who eats both vegans and vegetarians.

Lipozomes – like erogenous zones but easier to locate in the dark.

Healthy lifestyle – doing things that will either make you live longer, or make you so bored you just seem to be living longer.

Diet guru – a sado-masochist with a book deal.

Health food – nondescript stuff packaged in recycled paper that you could get for a quarter of the price in the rabbit section of your pet shop.

Nautilus – a torture chamber made to sound like a Greek god in the hope that you won't notice the pain when your testicles get trapped in the weights.

Dumb-bells – women who think that spending two minutes on the running machine and an hour in the jacuzzi will make them fit.

Crouching tiger, hidden dragon – a herbal enema.

Macrobiotic – a very big word to describe a diet that could not satisfy an amoeba.

Crystals – what comes out of your rear end after a week on a detox diet.

Addendum. Contrary to previous editions, pigeonholing, monkey-spanking and tit-rubbing are not legitimate keep-fit exercises after all.

CHAPTER 1

All about dieting

Dieting may be an almighty waste of time, but it's best to know your enemy.

Dietary tip no. 1 – if you're in a disco and the ultraviolet light makes your bones glow it's time to stop.

Recommended reading:

Think Yourself Thin, Poor and Destitute; Be a Size 10 in One Day by Changing the Labels in Your Clothes; The Hip and Thigh Diet: 50 Ways to Cook Them.

Don't go on a 28-day diet.
All you lose is four weeks.

The Zone – a diet that cuts
out all carbohydrates.

The Parking Zone – a diet
that cuts out all human
kindness and, if you're lucky,
certain body parts too.

Definition of a diet that works: any diet someone else is on.

Try food combining – that's where you combine eating food with throwing up.

Male diet rules:

1. Never eat anything that didn't die surprised.
2. Pork scratchings count as both roughage and carbohydrates . . . oh, and pudding if you're desperate.
3. The only way to really watch your weight is to lie on your back in front of a mirror. (NB: at a push, a TV will do.)

'Light lunch' – female: salad, a roll, a glass of water and an apple; **male:** two pints, bag of nuts, no crisps.

What diet food packs never say:

- ■ Looks like cardboard, tastes like shit.
- ■ Over-priced crap for fatties with no willpower.
- ■ Your loss, our gain.

What the diet books never say:

- Follow this for a week and you'll wish you'd never been born.
- Only works on compulsive anorexics.
- Will only help you lose weight if you eat these pages instead of food.

Put yourself off your food when eating out – choose a table next to the gents.

Be disciplined. Don't eat between snacks.

All foods are bad for you except watercress and if you eat that all the time you'll go green. Welcome to the wonderful world of nutrition.

Female method of losing 10lb: cut food intake down to a strict 1,000 calories a day, eat no chocolate, cakes, bread, butter, cream or sugar, go to the gym every day, start walking to work, cry at night because you're so hungry, snap at everyone at work because you're so hungry, finally lose weight after three months of misery. Put it back on the week after.

Male method of losing 10lb: eat ten kebabs, throw up.

32

Female diet rule no. 1:
Anything you eat from
someone else's plate does
not have calories –
particularly if it's chips.

Female diet rule no. 2:
Calories saved by having a
side salad and no potatoes
are enough to compensate
for those in two bottles of
Chardonnay and a Tequila
Sunrise.

Female diet rule no. 3:
Saying 'no thanks, I'm on a
diet' ten times in a day uses
up enough calories to allow
you a Kit-Kat by tea-time.

CHAPTER 2

Health and beauty tips for under a fiver

Looking good doesn't have to cost a lot of money. Well, it does, but seeing as you bought the book . . .

If you place cucumber slices over your eyes to reduce swelling, remember they can be reused later to make cucumber sandwiches for people you don't particularly like. This also applies to yogurt facial masks and anchovy earplugs.

Why pay good money for silicone implants? Shove two condoms filled with salad cream down your blouse and pray he doesn't get frisky.

Don't worry about minor wrinkles and stretch marks. Simply wear more revealing tops and men will hardly notice anything else . . . at least until another pair jiggles into view.

Save money on expensive
anti-wrinkle cream by simply
never going out again.

Always be seen in the company of people significantly uglier than yourself. That way, if you all get drunk and sleep with strangers, the cries of horror from adjoining rooms will wake you early enough to slip away unnoticed.

Make your own smudge-free lipstick by covering your mouth in a layer of Clingfilm. It works fine and also helps you get into late-night fetish parties.

Skincare ranges the Body Shop rejected:
- Extract of Nettle suppositories
- Eau de Stilton Bleu
- One-a-day Leeches

Cut-price zinc supplement: lick the pipes that lead to the hot tap.

Did you know, matchsticks make ideal dumb-bells for anorexic supermodels?

Save Greenpeace time and money by blockading your own house and hanging a sign from your window reading 'Cosmetics made me the freak I am!'

Jogging can be made more amusing by attaching humorous stickers to your arse. Suitable examples include 'My other buttock's a Porsche' or 'Honk if you're about to hit me from behind.'

Drink at least eight glasses of water a day. If you can't find water, try beer. It's all liquid, so who gives a . . .

Drink Aloe Vera juice every morning. It doesn't do you any good but it tastes so disgusting you won't want to eat anything else until tea-time.

Don't bother buying expensive women's magazines: they have twenty pages of recipes and five pages of diets.

Try naturism. It won't improve your looks, but it wouldn't half make the rest of us smile.

Cut-price peppermint tea.
Add two tablespoonfuls of
grass cuttings and one Polo
to boiling water. Allow to
simmer until green enough
to serve.

CHAPTER 3

Zen fattism

To be at peace with your inner rhino, you need a philosophy. Here are some we knocked up earlier.

Ask not what your country can do for you, ask, 'What's for dinner?'

The road to hell is paved with chicken wings.

Whoever said 'less is more' had obviously never heard of all you can eat restaurants.

Keep your enemies close but your popcorn closer still.

He who hesitates, escapes having to buy a round.

He who truly wants to get thinner, must visit a paint shop.

If there are fifty ways to
leave your lover, imagine
how many ways there are to
eat them.

Inside every thin woman is a fat one dying to get at the chocolate cake.

Remember, the phrase 'You can't be too rich or too thin,' was said before Posh Spice was invented.

The way to achieve true inner peace is to finish what you start. Finish the chocolate cake and half pound of fudge truffles you started and see just how much better you feel.

To maintain a healthy balance of mind and body, you should probably ignore the first and indulge the second.

If you're the wrong weight for your height, wear stilettos.

When choosing a yoga class
go for raspberry or hazelnut.

She who shops in
supermarkets must
exercise shelf-control.

To love yourself you must love your inner child: feed it with crisps and chocolates every three hours.

CHAPTER 4

DIY detox

All the celebrities have done detox, usually to save their careers or stay out of jail. Now you can do the same without the expense. Here's how.

DIY Acupuncture – Stand in the vicinity of the pub dartboard during a brewery-sponsored novices' darts tournament.

60

DIY Tantric Sex – Make sex last for eleven hours by simply having a damn good sleep in the middle.

DIY Colonic Irrigation – Take two chicken vindaloos and then stare at a photo of Anne Widdecombe.

DIY Nicotine Patches –
When you've finished your
cigarette, Sellotape the butt
to your arms. A 40-a-day
smoker will be unable to put
on his shirt by the end of the
day, thus restricting his
ability to get to the
tobacconist.

When kicking heroin, don't try and do it in the frozen foods section of Asda. Contrary to popular belief, Bernard Mathews did not invent cold turkey.

DIY Natural Childbirth –
Don't tell anyone you're nine
months pregnant, then go
down the water slide at
Disney World. (NB: close your
legs at the bottom unless
you fancy giving birth to a
bungee jumper.)

64

DIY Feng Shui – Hire a babysitter you hardly know for the night. When you return, many items of furniture will have been moved around and the hi-fi, TV and video will be missing.

DIY Hypnotherapy – Wait at pelican crossings watching the flashing amber light until you lapse into a deep meditative state or are hit by a car. Either way, you'll end up with the repressed memory of someone stealing your wallet.

DIY Chiropractic – Curl up inside a tumble dryer and get someone else to switch it on. When you hear strange cracking noises in your spine, pay the other person £50 and say you'll see them next Tuesday.

DIY Cosmetic Surgery –
Take a train to Glasgow and
get involved in a fight. Your
features will be rearranged
free of charge and wrinkles
will look far less prominent
next to the knife wounds.

DIY Collagen Implants – Take another train to Glasgow, and accuse the first man you see of being a poof. Voilà – instant swollen lips, eyes and cheekbones, plus a photographic souvenir of your new face, taken by the police.

DIY Organic Purge – sit on a piece of cheese and swallow a mouse.

Chapter 5

Fitness tips for slobs

Not everyone wants to win races. Some of us are happy to make it to the armchair.

Exercise for the slothful
- jumping to conclusions
- wrestling with your conscience
- running a temperature

Using the rowing machine for hours on end will not make you look like Steve Redgrave. It will make you look like someone who can't find the off switch and is gradually rowing himself to death.

Give toddlers a taste of their own medicine by weeing in the swimming pool just before they overtake you.

If you listen to music while jogging, try to find something that matches your natural rhythm. Suitable tracks include 'The Last Waltz' by Engelbert Humperdinck and Schubert's 'Unfinished Symphony'.

Never agree to meet
prospective business
partners at the squash
court. Squash is a stupid game,
where one player wins and
the other dies.

Why watch your calories when it's so much more fun to watch someone else's? For instance, try hanging round the fridge shaking your head if anyone tries to eat anything. Or stand in the supermarket with a big sign saying 'Mr Kipling ruins lives'.

True sizes:
size 18 = goddess
size 16 = normal
size 14 = nicely rounded
size 12 = bit on the
skinny side
size 10 = get real!
size 8 = freak of nature!

Cut-price kick-boxing:
spend an hour kicking every
cardboard box you can find
in your local supermarket.

When circuit training, always use the right equipment in strictly the right order. For example, the rowing machine comes after the treadmill but before the heart defibrillator and the ambulance ride to intensive care.

In a restaurant, if you must have a dessert, have it without cream. If they don't serve cream have it without custard instead.

Get exercise and boost your confidence at the same time: run round to all your old boyfriends and shout out their inadequacies through their letterboxes.

Boost your immune system – eat a bit of everything that's bad for you every morning, particularly fat, sugar and carbohydrates. A cream doughnut a day keeps the doctor away.

Keep fit by going to the gym every morning. Pull and push and strain and sweat until someone comes down and opens the door for you.
Then go home.

CHAPTER 6

Refuting fitness mantras

If someone's mantra is getting up your nose, you'd better fight back with one of your own.

'The key to fitness is a trim stomach.'
'Yeah, but the key to happiness is a full one.'

'Every day is a chance to
  succeed.'
*'Every night is a chance to
  concede.'*

'Push the envelope!'
*'Aww, can't I just lick the
  stamp?'*

'My body is a temple.'
*'Oh, is that why you charge
for entry?'*

'A healthy body means a
   healthy mind.'
*'Excuse me, you're jogging on
   my pizza.'*

'If you can pinch more than
an inch you're
overweight.'
*'If you can grab more than a
slab, you're asking for a
slap.'*

'Early to bed and early to
    rise, makes a man . . .'
'. . . *single and not getting
    any sex?*'

'My body is a temple.'
*'My body is a mosque – who
do you think the
neighbours are more
nervous about?'*

'Every morning I do fifty
sit-ups and go for a jog.'
'And every morning I let you.'

'I have a low tolerance for
dairy products.'
*'I have a low tolerance for
ugly people, but do you
see me complaining?'*

CHAPTER 7

Excuses for not having a healthy lifestyle

*Our philosophy –
No pain, no pain.*

Look, if I wanted to pay
£1.50 for a bottle of water,
I'd go to Lourdes.

I suffer from a weak bladder and they won't let me in the swimming pool.

I know I should eat fewer deep fried Mars Bars, but my Chinese herbalist tells me it all balances out with enough powdered rhino horn.

93

My problem isn't drinking too much, it's throwing up too little.

My bank manager told me he can't give me a second mortgage to finance my gym membership.

I've tried acupuncture, but with all the heroin I do there wasn't room for any more needles . . .

I'm allergic to Lycra, Spandex and Sweat.

I used to be an Olympic athlete – going to an ordinary gym would be a humiliation for me.

I tried giving up smoking, but the tobacco companies kidnapped my family.

Look, if I wanted more anabolic steroids in my system I'd sleep with a Gladiator.

I have a very good life insurance policy which I've left to charity – if I croak, half the Third World gets dinner.

Saturated fats? That's just something the CIA made up to scare Elvis.

I read somewhere that Fat was the new Thin and Horizontal the new Vertical. Do you think that's right?

Look, if you can 'feel the burn' you're obviously not holding your cigarette properly.

One woman's lard-arse is
another man's love-handles.

I'm a work of art – don't blame me because they haven't found the right frame yet.

I'm not anti-fitness, I'm pro-sloth.

CHAPTER 8

Fitness fads and fashions

Did you know, a new fad is invented every eight seconds and kills someone twelve seconds later? Here are a few coming your way soon.

Tai Dai – A long-winded form of Tai Chi, very popular in Wales.

The Marlon Brando Diet –
You're not allowed to eat
more than two endangered
species into extinction per
day.

Tantric Sleep – Render yourself instantly unconscious for eleven hours or more at a time. As practised by train drivers, students attending lectures and most of the cast of *Crossroads*.

The Viagra Diet – You're allowed to eat anything you can balance on the end of an erection.

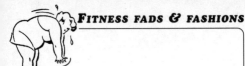

The Vanessa Diet – Hugely popular diet that does seem to achieve miraculous results. Unfortunate side effects include crying a lot on *Big Brother* and developing twice as many irritating habits as before.

The Happy Camper – Lose weight the celebrity way, by mincing around on prime-time television for a lot of money. As used by Graham Norton, Julian Clary and Dale Winton.

The California Workout –
Jump, stretch, push past the max.

The Brixton Workout –
Smash, grab, push past the shop assistant and leg it.

The Ab-Original –

Another abdominal workout machine, which doubles as a didgeridoo. As advertised by Rolf Harris.

Hyper-Organic Vegan Diet – A radical form of vegetarianism, which involves only eating things that have committed suicide. This includes most over-ripe fruit, nuts and some very depressed cows who lost close friends during the foot and mouth crisis.

The Jeffrey Archer Diet –
Possibly the most successful
of the celebrity diets, due to
its simplicity. When someone
asks you how much weight
you've lost, say something
like '300lb in three weeks'. If
they point out that this is
simply impossible, sue them
and get your wife to claim
she actually saw it happen.

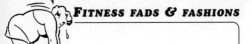
Apricot Anal Scrub – A bit like facial scrub, only you can't test it down the Body Shop.

CHAPTER 9

Things you don't want to hear during . . .

Aargh! The health and fitness nightmare has just begun. Oh, no, it's all right. You just fell asleep in your chair after a particularly cheesy cheeseburger with double fries and extra-thick milkshake.

Liposuction

Accept this sacrifice, O Lord Beelzebub!

Hey! Who's got the camera? Get a load of this freak of nature!

So everyone's washed their hands, right? No? Well, just wipe them on your overalls, that'll do.

Colonic Irrigation

Hey, I can see your house from down here!

I don't want to alarm you, but I think we've found Shergar.

Aerobics
'The Flight of the Bumblebee'.
'Grandad'.
'Smack my Bitch Up'.

The Health Farm

Hello – welcome to the most
   boring two weeks of your
   life.

Today we will be serving a
   lightly salted lettuce leaf
   followed by Twiglets made
   from real twigs.

And it's party night tonight!
   We'll have country dancing
   with fizzy water, fruit
   juice, nettle tea and raw
   carrot nibbles for
   refreshments. Isn't that
   exciting?

Rehab

Just a warning, our guard dogs have been trained to kill at the smell of vodka.

Great news! Keith Chegwin, Tara Palmer-Tomkinson and Vanessa Feltz are joining our group today.

Congratulations on kicking your addiction. By way of celebration, the staff will now get pissed and stoned while you watch.

Circuit Training

The bench press? Yes, it's over where that big guy has been lying for half an hour sweating on the leather.

Excuse me . . . are your eyes supposed to bulge like that?

Yoga

And now that you are
  trapped in the inverse
  lotus position, my healing
  hands will massage your
  supple young body . . .
No, I am not exactly a trained
  Yogi, but I am naked
  under this kaftan . . .

Hypnotherapy

When you awake you will feel a powerful attraction to your therapist . . .

I see, so in your dream you are made of chocolate, running up a chocolate hill and being chased by a chocolate tiger . . . I'm afraid it will take many more expensive sessions to interpret what you are truly seeking . . .

Cosmetic Surgery

Hi, welcome back from the anaesthetic – now tell me again . . . was it Annie Lennox or Lennox Lewis you wanted to look like?

Of course we're well known – Michael Jackson swears by us . . . well, at us, mainly.

Feng Shui

No, the furniture's fine, but
I'm afraid you'll have to
move the whole house.

Oh, I'm sorry . . . but
honestly, fresh water
flowing through your PC
really is good for it.

Here's my invoice – and no,
rearranging the figures is
not an option.

Four weeks into a crash diet

Hey, guess what . . . they've just discovered cholesterol is good for you!

Actually, I've changed my mind – it's not your figure I dislike, it's your personality . . .

OK, Tubby, this is the police! Put your hands on your head, and move away from the Häagen-Dazs . . .

Joining the Gym

Thank you for signing the direct debit. You'll be amazed how many pounds you'll lose over the next year.

. . . and here's your personal trainer, Olga. She's eighteen stone, eats rivets for breakfast and has a grudge against men.

Born the only poor black child of a middle-class Asian family, **Mike Anderiesz's** chronic lack of attention was always attributed to learning difficulties. He struggled at primary school till well into his thirties until renowned therapist Dr Howard Mutherfunk diagnosed the shocking true problem.

'I honestly think this is the most complacent man I have ever met,' he wrote. 'He drinks, he smokes, he's single, he's congenitally lazy, he's frankly unemployable – he really doesn't give a shit.' Anderiesz now delights audiences with his lectures, books and comedy coughing fits and is the CEO of 'Whatever', a support group for the chronically apathetic.

Jasmine Birtles' strict diet and exercise regime has meant she has often been compared to Pinochet, not least because of her fondness for attaching electrodes to people's genitals. Nutrition is her middle name, which caused some problems at her christening in Croydon. She has written several books on health issues including the seminal *Battenburg – The Man and His Cake*, and *Hermann Goering, His Struggle with Cellulite*. Since she hit eighteen Jasmine has had extensive plastic surgery and now looks exactly the same as she did as a student, except that she cannot swivel her eyeballs.